ANIMALS

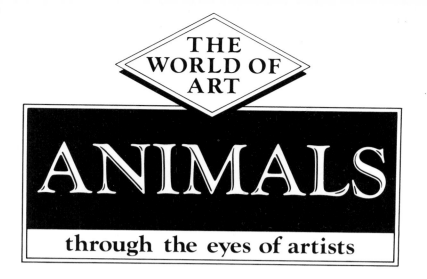

THE WORLD OF ART

ANIMALS

through the eyes of artists

28.12.61.

Reproduced by kind permission of Mademoiselle C Hutin

Wendy and Jack Richardson

MACMILLAN

First published 1989

Published by Macmillan Children's Books
A division of MACMILLAN PUBLISHERS LTD.
Houndmills, Basingstoke, Hampshire RG21 2XS and London

Companies and representatives throughout the world

Picture research by Faith Perkins

Printed in Italy

British Library Cataloguing in Publication Data

Richardson, Wendy
Animals
1. Visual Arts, to 1981. Special subjects: Animals –
For children
I. Title II. Richardson, Jack III. Series
704. 9′432′09

ISBN 0-333-47567-4

Photographic acknowledgements
The authors and publishers wish to acknowledge with thanks the following photographic sources:

cover: The Elephant Bath – The Victoria and Albert Museum, London
La Colombe – Reproduced by kind permission of Mademoiselle C Hutin (Appollot Photographie) piii
Rosa Bonheur – The Metropolitan Museum of Art, New York, Gift of the artist in memory of Rosa Bonheur pvi
The Animals Entering the Ark – Reproduced by gracious permission of Her Majesty Queen Elizabeth The Queen Mother p9
Bassano – The Prado, Madrid (Giraudon) p8
Rock Art, The Meads – Natal Museum, Pietermaritzburg p10-11
Domestic Fowl – Reproduced by kind permission of His Imperial Highness p13
The Fisherman Fresco, Thera (Ancient Art and Architecture Collection) p15
Young Bull – Mauritshuis, The Hague (Bridgeman Art Library) p16-17
Egyptian Hunting Scene – The British Museum (Michael Holford) p18-19
Battle of Anghiari – The Louvre, Paris (The Mansell Collection) p21 (bottom)
The Lion Hunt – Alta Pinakothek (Artothek) p21 (top)
Rubens – Private Collection (The Bridgeman Art Library) p20
The Horse Fair – The Metropolitan Museum of Art, New York, Gift of Cornelius Vanderbilt, 1887 p22-23 (top)
Horse Frieze – (Ancient Art and Architecture Collection) p22-23 (bottom)
Rosa Bonheur – The Metropolitan Museum of Art, New York, Gift of the artist in memory of Rosa Bonheur, 1922 p22
The Jockey – Victoria and Albert Museum, London (The Bridgeman Art Library) p25
Toulouse-Lautrec – Musée des Augustines, Toulouse p24
Torero Soulevé – Reproduced by kind permission of Mademoiselle C Hutin (Appollot Photographie) p26-27
Picasso – Gallatin Collection, Philadelphia Museum of Art © DACS 1988 (The Bridgeman Art Library) p26
Travoys with Wounded Soldiers – Imperial War Museum, London (The Bridgeman Art Library) p28-29
Spencer – The Tate Gallery, London p28
The Giraffe – Biblioteca Ambrosiana, Milan p30-31
Squirrels in a Chennar Tree – India Office Library, London. Reproduced by courtesy of th Trustees of the British Museum p33
The Hare – Albertina, Vienna (The Bridgeman Art Library) p35
Dürer – The Louvre, Paris (The Bridgeman Art Library p34
The Elephant – Reproduced by courtesy of the Trustees of the British Museum p36-37
Rembrandt – The Iveagh Bequest, Kenwood House, London (The Bridgeman Art Library) p36
The Green Monkey – The Walker Art Gallery, Liverpool p39
Stubbs – National Portrait Gallery, London p38
The Mandrill – Museum Boymans van-Beuningen, Rotterdam © COSMOPRESS, Geneva/DACS, London 1988 p41
Kokoschka – Museum of Modern Art, New York © COSMOPRESS, Geneva/DACS, London 1988 p40
The Captive Unicorn – The Metropolitan Museum of Art, New York (Ancient Art and Architecture Collection) p43
The Elephant Bath – The Victoria and Albert Museum, London p45
Matisse – Private Collection © Succession Henri Matisse DACS 1988 (The Bridgeman Art Library) p46
L'Escargot – The Tate Gallery, London © Succession Henri Matisse DACS 1988 (The Bridgeman Art Library) p47

The publishers have made every effort to trace the copyright holders, but if they have inadvertently overlooked any, they will be pleased to make the necessary arrangement at the first opportunity.

Introduction

This is a book of pictures of animals. Some of the pictures are very old and some of them were made quite recently. They come from all over the world. Some are paintings, some are drawings, some are embroideries, some are prints. Some come from books, some are on walls and some are made to hang on walls. They look very different, but they have one thing in common. They were made by people who had an idea about animals and thought that the best way to share their idea with us was through a picture. So this is a book for you to look at.

The pictures tell how the artists felt about animals. We humans love animals, but we also fear them. We use them by making them work for us, and we eat them. We tell stories about them, we have fun with them. We find animals fascinating so we study the way they live. We also hunt them and are cruel to them.

All these ideas have been expressed by artists. You will see how differently animals have made them feel, and you will feel different emotions as you look at the pictures. Some of the pictures may shock you, others make you feel angry. Some may make you curious, and others fill you with joy. Look carefully and see how you feel about each picture.

The Metropolitan Museum of Art, New York. Gift of the artist in memory of Rosa Bonh

Contents

The Animals Entering the Ark

Oil on canvas 118 × 170 cm
Jacopo Bassano (da Ponte)

LIVED:
c.1510/18-1592

NATIONALITY:
Italian

TYPE OF WORK:
Religious and animal paintings. The first landscapes in European painting

The Prado, Madrid

Jacopo Bassano was the father of a family of painters. They worked together from one studio, and shared an interest in painting animals. It is often difficult to know exactly whose work is whose in the family.

Nearly all painters in the sixteenth century chose religious or historical subjects. The Bassano family were among the first to break away from the tradition and to paint the natural world around them. They painted the animals and scenery of the Italian countryside.

A real interest in animals

This painting is an example of the way artists at that time were struggling to make the sort of pictures they wanted. It is a religious work, telling the story of Noah and the flood. It is a very good choice for a painter who was interested in animals. Look carefully at the animals as they go into the ark two by two. You will probably be able to tell which of them the painter had seen many times and which of them he had not often seen or had only heard about. One or two have never existed at all! At the time that this picture was painted, many people may have thought that all these animals were real.

Humans and animals

The story of the flood reminds us that we are animals too and share the Earth with them. Bassano sets Noah and his family right amongst the animals, pushing and pulling them into the ark. Meanwhile the sky is darkening with threats of the storm that is to come.

Rock Painting of Eland

Earth colours on natural rock
Artist unknown

DATE:
c.AD 1700

PLACE:
The Meads, Southern Drakensberg,
South Africa

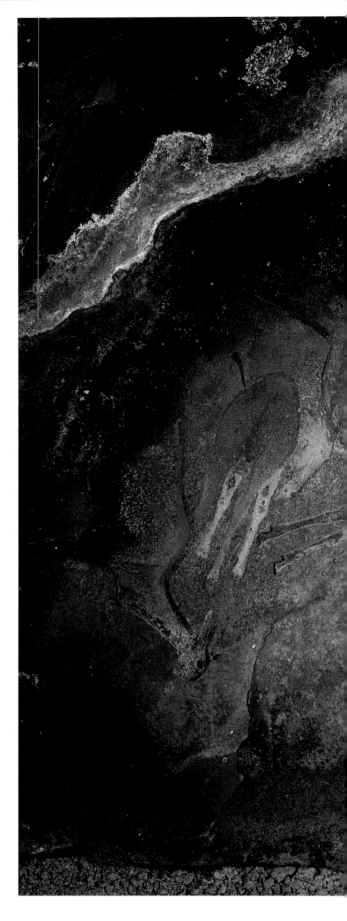

No one is sure who painted this picture. There are thousands of paintings in the same style on rocks in southern Africa. Archaeologists believe that they were probably painted by the ancestors of nomadic Bushmen peoples, some of whom live today in the Kalahari desert.

Paintings in the sunlight

Compared with some of the rock paintings found in Europe, these African paintings are recent. They were probably painted no more than two or three hundred years ago, but others like them are as much as 20 000 years old. Unlike the European paintings, which are found deep in caves, these paintings are all in rock shelters, open to the sunshine.

This painting was found in Southern Drakensberg. It was painted on the underside of a small overhanging rock. It was not found at a site where people lived, but in a place specially chosen for painting. It shows a wonderful herd of eland, which are a sort of antelope. These animals were of special importance in the religious mythology of the San peoples, and these are the animals which they painted most often.

Techniques

The paintings have great liveliness and strength, and were obviously painted by someone who had watched eland and knew how they lived. The animal drawing is very carefully observed. The colour range included black, yellow, brown and red. The paints were made from crushed rocks, earth and burnt materials. These were sometimes mixed with the blood and the hair of the animal being painted, and this mixture may have had magical meaning.

Many thousands of these paintings are still to be found where they were painted, but this one has been removed, on its rock, to a museum in Natal for safe keeping.

Domestic Fowl

Ink and colours on silk 143 × 80 cm
Itô Jakuchû

LIVED:
1716-1800

NATIONALITY:
Japanese

Itô Jakuchû wanted to make a survey of plants and animals for the Sokokuji Temple where he worshipped as a Buddhist. This painting is one of a set of thirty entitled *The Colourful World of Living Beings*. It is painted on dyed silks.

The animals in the paintings

The work contains no large animals and no human beings. The artist preferred to paint birds and fish, insects and plants. However, he did suggest that humans were around by painting domestic animals, gardens and crops.

There are more cockerels and hens in the paintings than any other creature. They must have been great favourites of Itô Jakuchû's for he kept them in his own backyard. In this picture they form a wonderful pattern of living colour. At the same time the picture shows very careful painting of the birds. The shapes of the feathers have particularly attracted the painter's attention with their mottled colours and their glossiness.

Painting on silk

The picture is painted on silk which has been dyed a warm brown colour, and our eyes travel down a vibrant zig-zag of scarlet cockscombs. Black and white balance each other. Yellow legs and browns in the feathers add to a richness which hardly seems possible when so few colours are being used.

When the animal paintings were finished Itô Jakuchû added a *tryptych* (a set of three paintings). Perhaps they were meant to suggest to followers of the Buddhist religion that all life, animal as well as human, is holy. This set of paintings is considered to be amongst the greatest pieces of Japanese painting.

The Fisherman

Natural colours on plaster
Artist unknown

DATE:
c.2000 BC

PLACE:
Santorini Island, Greece

This picture is a wall painting or *fresco*. It was found in the remains of an ancient city called Akroteri on the island of Santorini. The island is near Crete in the Mediterranean Sea. The city was destroyed by a volcanic eruption about 1550 BC and its ruins were covered in dust and ashes. Archaeologists began work there in 1967. They have uncovered many beautifully painted rooms, some showing plants, some animals and some human activity.

When Akroteri was a living city, it was an unusual place as far as painting was concerned. In the rest of Greece only the most important buildings were richly decorated. In this city the homes of the citizens were also painted. Artists seem to have had more freedom in Akroteri. Their work is more natural and they paint a greater variety of subjects than has so far been found elsewhere. Of course it may well be that our knowledge is incomplete. In the future archaeologists may find evidence to show that such painting was common in other cities of ancient Greece.

The room of the fishermen

This painting is one of a pair which were found in the same room. The piece of plaster on which it was painted had come away from the wall but the painting was not damaged. Both paintings are of fishermen holding strings of fish. Unfortunately the other panel is badly damaged. The fishermen are young and strong, and carry their catches with pride. The fish are caught up with a string through their mouths. The colours are bright and the fish still look fresh from the sea.

It is thought that this is the first painting in Greek art to show an adult naked. The blue hair, which is found in several of the Santorini paintings, seems to have been used to show young people.

Techniques

The picture was painted directly on to the wall. Sometimes the painters worked on wet plaster (*fresco*) and sometimes on dry plaster (*fresco secco*). First, grids were made to mark out the paintings and a plan was drawn. The colours were made by crushing minerals, and five basic colours were used, blue, orange, white, black and red. Many shades were mixed from these basic colours.

Young Bull

Oil on canvas 235.5 × 339 cm
Paulus Potter

LIVED:
1625-54

NATIONALITY:
Dutch

TYPE OF WORK:
Animal painting

Paulus Potter had only a short life, but when he died at the age of twenty-nine he was already well known and his work was very popular. He was the son of a painter, and lived and worked in Holland. He painted the Dutch countryside, with its flat meadows and its wild flowers. Most of all he loved to paint the cattle that grazed in the meadows. This picture is very large – the animals are almost life size.

The eye of the countryman

Potter painted these animals with great care, and he showed them just as they were, ordinary, lumbering farmyard animals. He observed them in close detail, almost as if he wished to paint every hair of their coats. This young bull with his fluffy matted head and his nervous strength looks out of the painting warily. Beside him the mature animal looks on without interest, and has the placid stare of domestic cattle.

Potter painted with a countryman's eye, though he lived in towns and cities, including Amsterdam. The world he shows is the real world of the farmer, not the sentimental view of the visitor from the city. He also studied the wild plants of the meadows and painted them with as much attention to detail as he gave to the animals. He seemed not to have been as interested in painting people as in painting animals. The man in this painting, who may be the cowherd, looks rather strange. He seems to have rather short legs. Perhaps he is standing in a ditch.

An amusing touch in this painting is the painter's signature. It is carved, graffiti-style, on the meadow fence.

The Mauritshuis, The Hague

Egyptian Hunting Scene

Watercolour on plaster 97.8 cm at its widest point
Artist unknown

DATE:
c.1400 BC

PLACE:
Egypt

Over three thousand years ago this picture was painted on the wall of a chamber in a tomb, in the ancient city of Thebes. Three people, a man, a woman and a child, are in a boat on the River Nile. Fish swim beneath them, but they are not fishing. They are hunting the birds that hide in the papyrus reeds. You can see the reeds at the left side of the picture. A tame cat, trained to help in the hunt, has jumped into the air and has grabbed a bird by the wing. A tame goose stands at the prow of the boat. The hunter holds a weapon in one hand, and three live birds, their wings flapping wildly, in the other. The air above the reeds is thick with many varieties of bird. It looks as if the hunt will be very successful. The man in the painting was Nebamun, an important court officer. He lived about one hundred years before Tutankhamun, who reigned in Egypt from 1361-1352 BC.

Techniques

Wall paintings are found not only in Egyptian tombs but also in homes and public buildings. Some were left unfinished and from them we know how they were painted. A grid was drawn out on the plaster, as was done on the island of Santorini. The figures were sketched in on the grid, allowing the painter to build up the design gradually. Then the background colours were painted, followed by the larger areas of the figures. Finally the details would be painted in on top of the previous colours.

Brushes were made from a straight twig or reed with the ends teased out. Paints, which were usually mixed with water but sometimes had some gum added to them, were made from natural materials. Reds and yellows were obtained from crushed soils, green from a hard stone called malachite and black from burnt substances. Six colours and many shades made by mixing them are found in the paintings.

The unknown painter

It seems that hunting wild fowl was a popular sport in ancient Egypt. Compare this painting with *The Lion Hunt* by Rubens on the following pages. Do you think that the unknown Egyptian painter thought about hunting in the same way that Rubens did? Do you react in the same way to both paintings? Which picture looks more like reality to you?

19

The Lion Hunt

Oil paint on canvas 249 × 375.5 cm
Peter Paul Rubens

LIVED:
1577-1640

NATIONALITY:
Flemish

Rubens was a Flemish painter who worked in the city of Antwerp in the country now known as Belgium. He spent eight years in Italy, from 1600-1608, studying the works of great painters. A painting by Leonardo da Vinci excited him so much that he made a copy of it.

When he returned to Antwerp, Rubens used this copy, called *the Battle of Anghiari* as a starting point for a painting of his own. Da Vinci had painted men fighting men, but Rubens' painting shows men fighting animals. However, the same strength and speed of movement are to be found in both pictures.

Power and excitement

This large painting has an immediate effect on most people. What are your feelings when you look at it? Rubens was expressing his ideas about passionate feelings such as fury and terror. He uses rich strong colours, reds, blacks and golds. They produce violent contrasts of light and darkness. Although there is actually very little blood to be seen in the picture, the impact is a very gory one.

The importance of design

It is not just the colour that makes the painting so strong and exciting. The way in which the men and animals fit together in a swirl of movement is just as important. The four huge horses, with twisted necks and flying hoofs, the men, armed with knives and spears, and the lions armed with teeth and claws, are parts of one great writhing monster-like shape. In the centre of the monster is the massive head of the lion, its claws tearing into the flesh of a horse, its teeth into the man it is pulling to the ground. Flailing human arms raise weapons and strike with all the force of bulging muscles. Everything in the picture is moving. Even the clouds are heaping and piling threateningly.

Each detail plays an important part in involving us in this picture. Eyes gleam, coats glisten with sweat. Faces are twisted in fear or anger. The sky is dark and the painting is lit by the strange heavy light that comes before a thunderstorm.

Rubens influences others

Rubens painted many pictures which show this power and vitality. Just as he had learnt from the works of good painters before him, so later painters were influenced by his work.

Alta Pinakothek

The Louvre, Paris

The Horse Fair

Oil on canvas 244.5 × 506.7cm

Marie Rosalie (Rosa) Bonheur

LIVED:
1822-1899

NATIONALITY:
French

TYPE OF WORK:
Animal paintings

The Metropolitan Museum of Art, New York, Gift of the artist in memory of Rosa Bonheur, 1922

Rosa Bonheur loved animals. When she was still a child she had a small zoo in her family home, which was a flat at the top of six flights of stairs. She even kept a goat, which had to be brought all the way down to ground level for a breath of fresh air.

As well as looking after her animals Rosa Bonheur started to draw and paint them. Her very first exercise book has animal drawings in it.

As she grew up Bonheur travelled to markets and to slaughter houses to draw and to gain knowledge of the animals she wanted to paint. It was unusual to find a woman in such places in those days. Bonheur was even more unusual. She insisted that she could not possibly work wearing the long full-skirted dresses that all women wore in the nineteenth century. So she persuaded the police to give her a special permit which allowed her to wear men's clothing for her work.

Strength and control

This very large painting, *The Horse Fair*, was one of the most popular paintings of its time. Like Rubens' painting, *The Lion Hunt*, this painting is full of power and excitement. It captures the wild free spirit of the animals. However, unlike the Rubens, Bonheur's is a cheerful painting. The strength of the animals is shown as something we might be joyful about, not as something to fear. The humans in the painting are not in danger from the animals' strength, they have control over it. For all the wildness and energy that Bonheur shows there is no sense of threat. The fair is an exciting but not a dangerous place to be.

Another picture in mind

The scene at the horse fair reminded Bonheur of something that she had already seen. The shapes of the people and the horses were like the carved stone friezes from the Parthenon of Athens.

Compare the painting with the photograph of the friezes. Can you see what Bonheur saw? Do you think the sculptor and the painter share an idea about people and horses?

The Metropolitan Museum of Art, New York, Gift of Cornelius Vanderbilt, 1887

The Jockey

Lithograph 51.5 × 36 cm

Henri de Toulouse-Lautrec

Musée des Augustines, Toulouse

LIVED:
1864-1901

NATIONALITY:
French

TYPE OF WORK:
Drawings, paintings and
lithographs, portraits and posters

Henri-Marie-Raymond de Toulouse-Lautrec-Monfa was born in Albi in southern France. His family were wealthy aristocrats. In two accidents when he was a teenager Toulouse-Lautrec broke bones in both legs. The bones stopped growing, so that when he was an adult Toulouse-Lautrec was only 137 cm tall.

His family shared two passions. They loved horse riding and they loved to draw. Unable to ride after his accidents, Toulouse-Lautrec persevered with his drawing and in 1882 he went to Paris to take lessons in painting.

Finding a style

Toulouse-Lautrec met many painters in Paris. He was interested in their work, but he developed a distinct style of his own. His pictures are like drawings, with strong outlines and flat blocks of thin colour. He also started to work in lithography which was a type of printing. A drawing was made on to a block of stone, then the lines of the drawing were cut away with acid. The surface of the block was covered with ink, and then cleaned, leaving the ink in the lines. The surface could then be printed on to paper. Toulouse-Lautrec became very well known for the lithographed posters he designed for the theatre.

A lithograph

This picture, *The Jockey*, is one of Toulouse-Lautrec's lithographs. His early experiences of horses and racing enabled him to draw the animals and their riders with real knowledge. It is a very simple picture, a coloured drawing, but very cleverly designed. The horses seem to move across the paper with thundering speed and it feels as if in a second they will be gone. The landscape through which they are racing is just a blur. The great haunches of the horse nearest to us power it forward. The horse's arching neck and narrow head are already distant from us. The pale colours the artist has used emphasise the dark lines of the drawing, while the effect of the jockeys' white shirts is startling.

Victoria and Albert Museum, London

Le Torero Soulevé

Oil on canvas 80 × 190 cm

Pablo Picasso

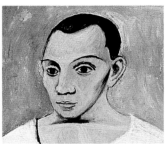

LIVED:
1881-1973

NATIONALITY:
Spanish, but lived most of his working life in France

TYPE OF WORK:
Painter, potter, sculptor, stage and film designer, print maker

Gallatin Collection, Philadelphia Museum of Art © DACS 1988

Pablo Ruiz y Picasso was a brilliant draughtsman and painter even as a child. By the time he was sixteen years old he had learned all that he could at the art schools in Spain. When he was nineteen he made his first visit to Paris. He settled there two years later, but returned to Spain frequently.

The tireless worker

Picasso was adventurous in his work and eager to explore new ideas. He gobbled up ideas from everywhere, seeing the world with a clear fresh eye. He worked tirelessly all his life. When he died in 1973, aged ninety-two, he had made thousands of drawings and paintings. He had filled 175 notebooks with sketches, observations and ideas, and it was upon this collection of information that he built his most important works.

The Spaniard in France

Though he lived most of his adult life in France, Picasso remained truly Spanish. He often went to watch bullfights in the arenas of southern France. He drew the toreadors, bulls and horses time and time again. He made the same accurate observations as other painters, but he turned those observations into something that was unique.

Conflict and pageant

Picasso sees the bullfight as part pageant and part contest. He paints it in the brilliant colours of a Mediterranean afternoon. Against the searing yellow of the arena sand he paints the bull in massive black. The toreador himself is deathly white against the bull's blackness. His tinselled suit catches the light. His cloak is a scarlet splash.

More than the camera

Picasso's pictures capture for us more than one view of the event. We see the bull from several angles. We see him front view, with distended nostrils. We see from the top of his head both his curling horns. An ear and an eye are drawn twice. It is as if Picasso is trying to show us the movement of the bull's head as it tosses the toreador. All the shapes are made as simple as possible so that we are not distracted from the drama of the moment.

Travoys with Wounded Soldiers

Oil paint on canvas 183 × 218.4 cm

Stanley Spencer

LIVED:
1891-1955

NATIONALITY:
British. During the 1914-18 war he served in the army in Greece

TYPE OF WORK:
Oil paintings, murals

The Tate Gallery, London

Stanley Spencer, an English artist, painted this picture in 1919. He painted at home in his cottage but he painted scenes from his real recent experience of war. From the war front he wrote a letter to Hilda Carline:

'...I was standing a little way from the old Greek church which was used as a dressing station and operating theatre and there were rows of travoys* of wounded and limbers† crammed full of wounded men. One would have thought the scene was a sordid one, a terrible scene, but I felt there was a grandeur...'

Perhaps Spencer re-read this letter when he came to paint the picture, for the scene is clearly the same one. The strong shapes of the mules, dark against the warm light of the makeshift operating theatre, and the converging lines of the poles of the travoys lead our eyes into the central open doorway. It is like a scene from the Christian nativity story, where the animals stand in the stable by the brightly lit figures of Joseph and Mary and the baby Jesus.

The letter to Hilda continued

'...all those wounded men were calm and at peace with everything, so the pain seemed a small thing with them.'

The colours of calmness

Spencer used autumnal colours, all very close in tone, rather than the bright splashes of red which he might have chosen to show the wounded men. These calm colours give use the feeling of peace which Spencer himself felt at the time. The lines of the picture are also orderly. There is no confusion, no rushing around, simply patient mules waiting quietly for their turn to approach the welcoming glow.

The eye of experience

This is an unusual picture of war, and one which could have been painted only by someone who saw and felt it. Spencer was a soldier (his duties involved working with the mules) but he made time to draw. Though many of his drawings were lost, some survived. They may have been useful when he painted this picture.

* **travoy** – a stretcher pulled by a horse.
† **limber** – a wooden trailer, usually for pulling guns.

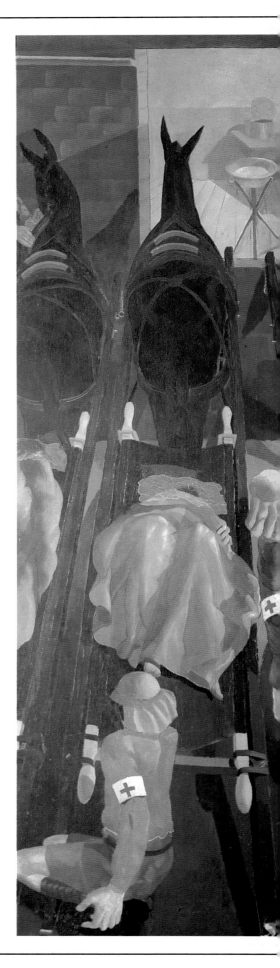

Bridled Giraffe

from the *Kitab al-Hayawan* (the *Book of Animals*)
Artist unknown

DATE:
Fourteenth century

PLACE:
Probably Syrian

This picture of a giraffe was painted to illustrate a book which had been written six hundred years earlier. The book was written by Abu 'Uthman 'Amr bin Bahr al-Jahiz who lived from 776-869.

There is very little Arab painting, because the holy book of Islam, the Qu'ran, forbids the making of images. However, in the twelfth, thirteenth and fourteenth centuries, in certain parts of the Islamic world, book illustration was not considered to be against the religious law. Illustrated copies of many books were made.

The *Book of Animals* is a collection of animal stories. We know that the author was one of the first writers to write books for ordinary people rather than for rich people or scholars but we know nothing about the illustrator of this copy.

A simple style

Despite the discoloration and the smudging that are the result of age, the simple flat figures hold our interest. The giraffe is strongly drawn. We are in no doubt that the painter was very familiar with this animal. The picture is well balanced. The spear, the giraffe's leg and the tall plant, and the lines of script above and below, make a frame to hold the action.

The giraffe looks as if it belongs to a rich person. It wears a bridle of gold, and an embroidered blanket covers its back. It even has golden bangles around its ankles. Can you imagine the story that the picture illustrates?

The importance of calligraphy

Since drawings were not often made in the Arab world, handwriting, or calligraphy, became an important art form. It is used to decorate books of all sorts and it is carved in stone on buildings, too. The script is very beautiful to look at, and flows from right to left in graceful curves. It would have been as important to the book illustrator to keep the graceful flow in the painting as it was to tell the story. Do you see any similarity between the pattern of the drawing and the pattern of the writing?

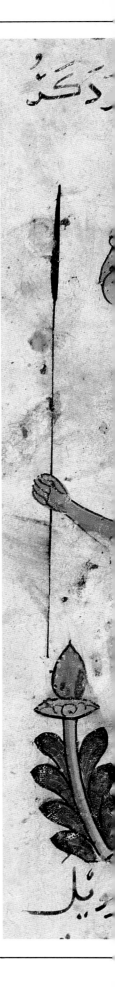

بالشريع والكذب سلة
من بني الناقة من يوق الحوش ومن لفقرة الوحشية ويين الد

الضباع وذلك انهم لمار اوا الاسهاب العار رشية اشتركاوبلنا

Squirrels in a Chennar Tree
Paint on paper
Abul Hasan

LIVED:
1589-1650

NATIONALITY:
Indian

TYPE OF WORK:
Portraits and animals

Abul Hasan lived and worked at the court of the Mughal emperors of India in the seventeenth century. He was one of many painters employed by the court to make records of important events and of the people at court. The Emperor Jahangir, who came to the throne in 1605, had many artists working for him, and he took a particular interest in their work. They not only painted pictures, but copied texts. Each artist was a specialist. Abul Hasan was best known for his skill as a portrait painter.

Here we see one of Hasan's animal paintings. Some critics now think it is so good that it rivals the animal paintings of Dürer and of the great Chinese artists.

Lightness and movement

The squirrels in the chennar tree are shown as very lively, quick moving animals. As they scamper from branch to branch, their lithe little bodies are balanced by their waving tails. Abul Hasan has arranged the squirrels in a circle. He is drawing our attention to the babies who poke their heads from a hole, reaching their noses towards their mother. It is the white patches on their stomachs and noses that catch our eye at first, then their bright dark eyes. The animals are at home in the dappled branches of the tree. The leaves are the strongest colours in the painting. They form a framework in which the squirrels play. If our eyes follow the line of the squirrels' tails, we seem to see them moving, their tails flicking. This is exactly how squirrels do dart among branches.

Harmony

The colours are very peaceful together, they do not contrast or clash. The sandy golden background allows us to see the animals and the tree quite clearly but does not conflict with them. There is a very close harmony at work.

The clever use of colour and the flowing composition capture for us a warm and happy moment as the squirrel family frisks.

The Hare

Water colour and gouache 25 × 22 cm

Albrecht Dürer

LIVED:
1471-1528

NATIONALITY:
German

TYPE OF WORK:
Engraving, jewellery, stained glass, paintings

The Louvre, Paris

Dürer was a highly skilled craftsman, a jeweller and engraver as well as a draughtsman and painter. He travelled widely and was intensely curious about everything that came his way. Dürer made drawings of all kinds of things, as if to help him to understand and analyse what he saw. When he was only thirteen he made a portrait of himself. It is the first self-portrait that we know of in European art.

Dürer's hare is probably the most popular animal picture ever. He painted it partly in watercolour, which is translucent – it allows light to pass through it. He also used gouache, which is a thicker, more opaque paint. The painting is tiny and the brush strokes with which the fur is painted are incredibly fine. The hare seems so life-like that we feel we might pick it up from the paper and stroke it.

The Elephant

Black chalk on paper 17.8 × 25.6 cm

Rembrandt van Rijn

LIVED:
1606-1669

NATIONALITY:
Dutch

TYPE OF WORK:
Oil paintings, mainly of people. Many portraits

The Iveagh Bequest,
Kenwood House, London

Like Dürer, Rembrandt suffered from endless curiosity about the natural world. He drew this elephant in Amsterdam when a travelling circus came to town. He may never have seen such a creature before. His chalk drawing wonderfully catches the elephant's shape and the way its skin hangs in wrinkles and folds. He manages to make us understand the colossal weight of the animal. We can almost feel the snake-like stretch of its sensitive trunk. With just a few strokes of his chalk Rembrandt makes a creature so real that we can imagine touching its leatheriness, and can see the doleful look in its eye.

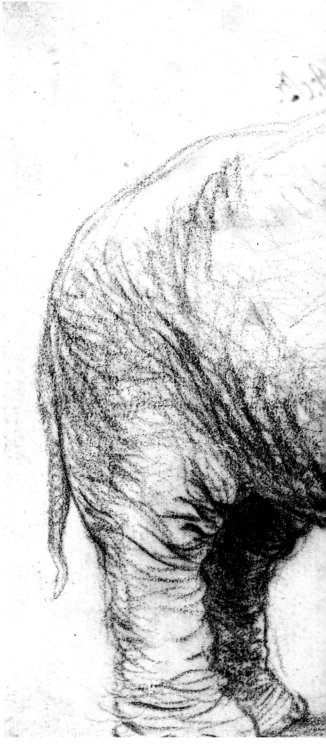

The Green Monkey

Oil on canvas 69.8 × 55.8 cm

George Stubbs

LIVED:
1724-1806

NATIONALITY:
British

TYPE OF WORK
Oil paintings of animals and book illustrations

National Portrait Gallery, London

George Stubbs was apprenticed to a painter in Liverpool at the age of fifteen, but he did not stay long as an apprentice. He left, and it seems that after that time he taught himself to paint. Stubbs became best known for his paintings of horses.

The age of discovery

Stubbs lived in an age of exploration and discovery. He was himself as much a scientist as a painter. He was particularly interested in the way in which the bones and muscles in human and animal bodies fitted together. This study is called anatomy. Stubbs lectured at a university on this subject and he illustrated several books about it.

Animals and plants were brought to Europe from all over the world at that time. Explorers wanted accurate records of their finds, but there were no photographs in those days. Stubbs was asked to paint a kangaroo which had been brought to England by a member of Captain Cook's expedition. Then he was asked by John Hunter, the owner of a growing museum and a menagerie, or zoo, to paint this picture of a monkey.

Stubbs the scientist

Stubbs saw the monkey in captivity in a land which was not its own. Yet he enables us to see a quick-moving and nervous wild creature, which might at any second take flight into the trees. He has painted the monkey looking directly at us, in the open, inquisitive way that monkeys have. It inspects us while we inspect it, and we can understand its anxiety.

Stubbs' scientific interest in the animal ensured that we see exactly what it looked like. The fur is painted so realistically that we can imagine what it would feel like to touch, and we can also imagine the bony little body beneath the skin.

Stubbs had never travelled outside Europe, and we can see the difference between his painting of the animal, which he could observe closely, and the trees which he had to imagine. The trees are based on the English woods which Stubbs knew well, but he changed them a little to make them look 'foreign'. He has used dark colours so that they do not disturb our study of the monkey.

Mandrill

Oil on canvas 127 × 102 cm

Oskar Kokoschka

LIVED:
1886-1980

NATIONALITY:
Born in Vienna, Austria. Kokoschka became a British citizen in 1947

TYPE OF WORK:
Oils and watercolours

Museum of Modern Art, New York
© COSMOPRESS, Geneva/DACS,
London 1988

Oskar Kokoschka studied the animals he painted very carefully. He visited London in 1926 and was given permission to work in the zoo when it was closed to the public. He has written about the experience,

> '. . . At night in the Monkey House, I painted a big, solitary mandrill, who profoundly detested me, although I always brought him a banana in order to make myself agreeable . . .'

What a contrast between the mandrill and Stubbs' little green monkey! Both are seen in captivity and both are being inspected, but Stubbs' monkey looks at us with a nervous curiosity, while Kokoschka's mandrill stares scornfully. He seems to be relaxed, but his teeth are bared. We should not go any closer. We can see quite clearly that the painter was wary of his hostile night-time companion.

Wild brush strokes

Kokoschka makes no attempt at the photographic realism that Stubbs achieved. His brush strokes do not try to give us fur to touch. Their wildness is intended to create excitement. With bold colours and bold marks he shows us the untamed animal. Like Stubbs he sets the animal in a tropical background, but the mandrill himself sits in a shadowy corner. He will not perform for us.

Unicorn in Captivity

Tapestry, wool with silk 368.3 × 251.5 cm
Artist unknown

DATE:
Late fifteenth century

NATIONALITY:
French or Flemish

Tapestries are pictures which are woven with wool, silk or linen thread. Occasionally there may be gold and silver threads in them too. They used to be very popular wall coverings in great houses and castles. They kept out the cold as well as being decorative.

The finest tapestries in the Middle Ages came from France and Flanders (now part of France, Belgium and The Netherlands.) This lovely picture of a solitary unicorn is the last in a set of six tapestries. The set shows the creature being hunted down and finally caught. We do not know where the tapestries were made and we do not know who made them.

The legendary unicorn

The unicorn is a mythical creature with the body of a swift horse, the tail of a lion and the beard of a goat. In the centre of its head is a single horn. Legend said that no animal could outrun the unicorn and so it could never be captured in the hunt. In the six tapestry scenes the story is told of how the unicorn was caught. It met a young girl, and lay down by her side with its head in her lap. In this last picture we see it fenced in. It has lost its freedom. It wears a collar and chain of gold by which it is tethered to a pomegranate tree. It sits in a meadow of flowers unable to escape.

Stories and symbols

The people of the Middle Ages delighted in the natural world of plants and animals. They also enjoyed stories and legends, and often their stories had hidden meanings. The story of the unicorn is full of such meanings. The unicorn himself, the most beautiful of creatures, may represent the Risen Christ, whilst the young girl represents the Virgin Mary.

The light of the world

The whole tapestry is rich and alive with colour. The picture seems to be lit magically from the unicorn with its pale coat. The slender trunk of the tree and the encircling fence glow in a golden light which catches the plants close by and then fades away to darkness.

A White Elephant

Silk embroidery
Artist unknown

DATE:
Eighteenth century

NATIONALITY:
Japanese

This elephant is not at all like Rembrandt's elephant. It is not a serious, closely observed animal. The drawing is more like a cartoon. It is a visual joke.

White elephants are extremely rare, and for thousands of years they were treated as very special. To be given one was like having a god living in your stables. In Thailand a white elephant was so special that even the King was not allowed to ride on it.

Keeping a white elephant was very expensive because it was not made to work. So to give an enemy a white elephant was sometimes seen as an easy way to make that person poor. We still talk of property that we do not really want as a 'white elephant'.

The skilful needle

We do not know who made this wonderful embroidery. It is worked in silk thread on a beautiful rich blue silk cloth. The artist did not know elephants very well. The feet and the tail belong to some other animal, but the mistakes do not matter. We are in no doubt which animal this is meant to be.

The elephant is enjoying itself. It smiles with real pleasure as its army of servants scrub its back and prepare its bath water. It has golden ladders and golden vessels, and it is held loosely on a golden chain by an admiring attendant. The elephant bends forward to help its servants who reach with long brushes or stretch dangerously down its slippery flanks. There is a pantomime feel to the picture. At any minute there may be a disaster.

The Japanese embroiderers of the eighteenth century were very skilful. This artist was able to draw with needle and thread the fine details and patterns of clothing and the large and wonderful elephant. Even the folds in the elephant's skin seem to be reflected in the way the silk has been stitched. The expressions on the faces of the attendants tell us that everyone is very happy.

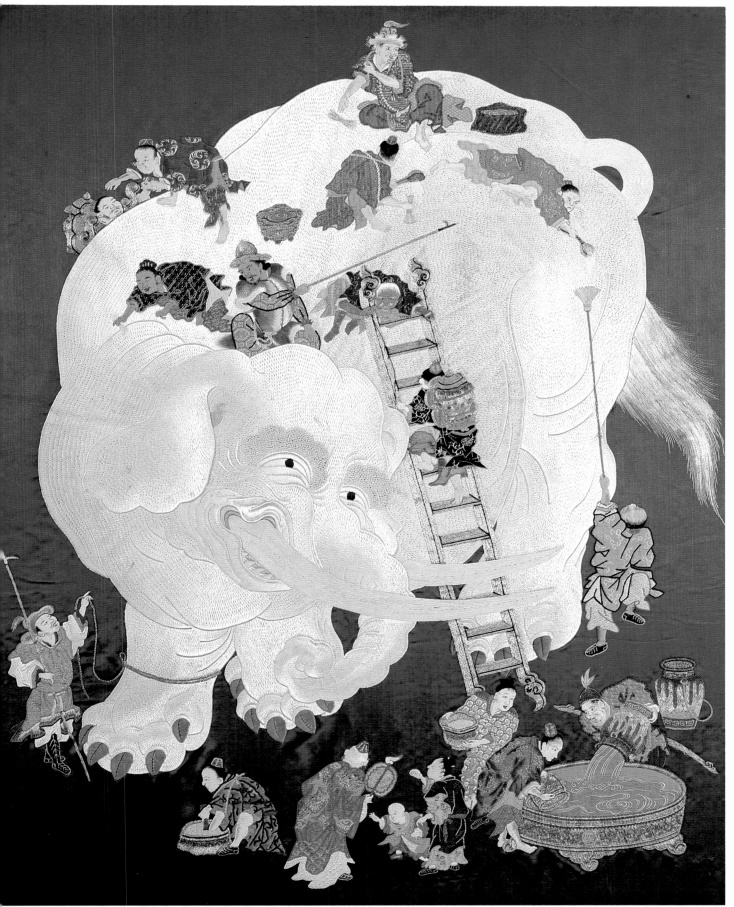

45

L'Escargot (The Snail)

Collage 286 × 287cm
Henri Matisse

LIVED:
1869-1954

NATIONALITY:
French

TYPE OF WORK:
Paintings and collages

Private Collection © DACS 1988
Succession Henri Matisse

You will have to look hard to find the snail in this picture. It is certainly not a carefully observed portrait. Henri Matisse, the artist who painted it, said that he wanted to, '….interpret nature and submit it to the spirit of the picture.' Can you think what he meant?

Matisse was one of a group of artists. They were determined to explore every possibility that colour and shape and texture could hold. They also set out to shock the world of artists and art critics, and the general public. They wanted to wake them up, to make them see the world as an exciting place full of surprises. They were so successful that they became known as Les Fauves (the wild beasts).

Moving colour

Matisse was interested in the effects of colours when they are placed next to each other. Some will appear to be further away from us than others. Some will make our eyes move quickly backwards and forwards between them. Some appear to sit restfully side by side, whilst others seem to overspill and merge.

Paper shapes

Matisse was interested by the spiralling shape of the snail. He used his knowledge of colour to make shapes cut out of paper appear like a snail. He wanted to make the spiral and he also wanted to create a vision of depth. Using only geometric shapes he tried to create a feeling of curves and solidity. Perhaps the rectangle of blue at the bottom represents a snail's body. Perhaps the square of green at the right represents its head. What do you think? Can you see now what Matisse meant by 'interpreting nature'? Do you think he has succeeded here?

Some ideas

For animal lovers

You may have read this book because you like animals. If so, perhaps you might try drawing them so that you can get to know them better. Remember how determined George Stubbs and Rosa Bonheur were? They wanted to find out exactly what animals were like. Drawing and painting helped them. It could also help you.

For picture lovers

You may have read this book because you like looking at pictures. Remember Rubens' excitement when he went to Italy? There is really nothing like seeing the real painting. A list at the front of the book tells you where to find those paintings which are on view to the public. They are in galleries all over the world so you will not be able to see them all. Your nearest gallery may have other works by the artists you like.

For those who want to have a go themselves

You may have read this book because you like to draw or paint. If so perhaps it has helped you to discover some of the secrets of picture making. All the work that is in the book is the result of hard thinking, lots of practice and above all very careful looking. Remember Picasso's notebooks? Perhaps you could start a notebook now. You could begin to collect the information that will help you to make your own ideas come alive in pictures.